Expeditions

in Reading

3

K12 Summit
CURRICULUM

Book Staff and Contributors

Kristen Kinney-Haines   *Director, English Language Arts*
Amy Rauen   *Director, Instructional Design*
Charlotte Fullerton   *Senior Media Editor*
Susan Raley   *Text Editor*
Tricia Battipede   *Senior Creative Manager, Cover Design*
Caitlin Gildrien   *Print Visual Designer, Cover Design*
Tim Mansfield, Alane Gernon-Paulsen   *Writers*

About K12 Inc.

K12 Inc. (NYSE: LRN) is driving innovation and advancing the quality of education by delivering state-of-the-art, digital learning platforms and technology to students and school districts across the globe. K12's award winning curriculum serves over 2,000 schools and school districts and has delivered millions of courses over the past decade. K12 is a company of educators providing online and blended education solutions to charter schools, public school districts, private schools, and directly to families. The K12 program is offered through more than 70 partner public schools, and through school districts and public and private schools serving students in all 50 states and more than 100 countries. More information can be found at K12.com.

K12

978-1-60153-570-2

Printed by Walsworth, Marceline, MO, USA, May 2020

Illustrations Credits

All illustrations © K12 unless otherwise noted.

Front Cover Matt Fedor.
8–9 Nicole Wong. **11, 13, 14** David Leonard. **17, 18, 20–21** Ian Joven. **25, 26–27, 28, 29, 30–31** Emma Gillette. **32–33, 34, 35, 36, 38–39, 40–41, 43, 44–45, 47** Billy Yong. **49, 50, 51, 53, 54, 55** Micha Archer. **57, 58, 59** Kristin Sorra. **63, 64, 65** Justin Hernandez. **67, 69, 71** Zhen Liu. **73, 74, 75, 77** Yevgenia Nayberg. **79, 80, 81, 83, 84–85** Andy Elkerton. **112–113** Nicole Wong. **114–115** Carolina Faría. **117** Jennifer Zivoin. **118–119** Charles Lehman. **124–125, 126, 127, 128, 129** Robert Meganck. **131, 132, 133, 135, 137, 139, 140, 141** Yu-Mei Han. **142–143** Sarolta Szulyovsky. **146–147, 149, 151** Mina Price.

Photo Credits

Cover and Interior Pattern Spiral turquoise background © Silmen/iStock.
89 Pole with too many wires. © mtcurado/iStock. **90–91** Eastern Shore of Maryland. © Joseph Sohm/Shutterstock. **93** Buried electric cable flag. © fstop123/iStock. **94–95** Prairie. © kool99/iStock. **96** Road closed sign. © CircleEyes/iStock. **99** Birds. © Branislav Novak/EyeEm/Getty Images. **100–101** Large pile of junk food. © mphillips007/iStock. **103** Fresh green beans. © loops7/iStock. **104–105** Eating. © monkeybusinessimages/iStock. **107** Sushi and maki. © Lordn/iStock. **108** Fun family mealtime. © Pekic/iStock. **110** Happy little girl with taco. © goce/iStock. **120–121** Snow. © LilKar/Shutterstock.

Text Credits

"April Rain Song" by Langston Hughes, from *The Collected Poems of Langston Hughes*. Copyright © 1994 by The Estate of Langston Hughes. Used by permission of Alfred A. Knopf, a division of Random House, Inc.

While every care has been taken to trace and acknowledge copyright, the editors tender their apologies for any accidental infringement when copyright has proven untraceable. They would be pleased to include the appropriate acknowledgment in any subsequent edition of this publication.

Expeditions
in Reading

K12 Summit
CURRICULUM

Contents

Weather, Weather Everywhere

Lessons Learned

Fables

The Wind and the Sun

adapted from a fable by Aesop

One day, the Wind and the Sun **exchanged** words about which was the stronger.

"I am the stronger," puffed the Wind. "See how I can send the black clouds flying through the sky."

"No doubt you are strong," was the Sun's gentle reply. "But how can you prove that you are stronger than I?"

"I can soon prove that," said the Wind. "You see that man walking along the road? Let us agree that whoever can make the man take off his coat is stronger."

"Agreed!" said the Sun. "You may try first."

So the Wind blew a fierce blast. It blew harder and harder. But the man only turned his back to the Wind and wrapped his coat more closely around him.

....

exchanged gave and received

In vain,
the noisy
Wind tried to
blow the man's
coat off. Then the
Wind said to the Sun, "It is
your turn to try now."

So the Sun sent some gentle rays down upon the
man. Soon the man became so warm that he was
glad to unbutton his coat.

By and by, he became so warm that he pulled off
his coat and hung it over his shoulder.

Thus, the gentle Sun proved to be stronger than
the noisy Wind. Gentle ways often prevail when
rough ones fail.

....

in vain without success

The Cruel Lion and the Clever Rabbit

Once upon a time in the Indian forest of Gir lived a cruel lion named Bhaksuraka. Bhaksuraka was strong and mighty. He was also always hungry.

Every night, Bhaksuraka would stalk the forest, looking for his dinner. The other animals scattered. They were afraid of the lion's huge teeth and enormous paws. The monkeys climbed high up into the treetops. The antelopes and peacocks hid themselves among the brush and held their breath, hoping Bhaksuraka wouldn't see them.

Night after night, a clever Rabbit watched the dinner dance in the forest. She heard Bhaksuraka's stomach rumble before the lion appeared. She poked her head out of the ground and watched the peacocks and antelope scatter. She listened to the rustle in the trees as the monkeys climbed higher and higher away from the lion. And she heard a cry when Bhaksuraka found something to eat.

One night, the Rabbit decided that enough was enough. She called the rest of the animals to a meeting under the tallest tree in the forest. "Bhaksuraka is a bully," the Rabbit told her friends. "I am tired of listening to his stomach rumble. I am tired of watching him stalk the forest. And I am tired of watching all of you run away in fear."

"But he is so big," one of the peacocks cried.

"And his teeth are so sharp!" an antelope said. Her friend nodded in agreement.

"And those paws," a monkey said, shaking his head from side to side. "One swipe and he would knock me out of the tree. And then I would be his dinner."

The Rabbit twitched her nose and looked at the animals gathered around her. "He may be stronger, but we can be smarter. I will speak to Bhaksuraka tonight."

The monkey paced back and forth in front of the Rabbit. "Aren't you scared he is going to eat you for his dinner?"

"I am a little scared," the Rabbit replied. "But I have a plan."

"Good luck," the antelope said. "You are very brave for being such a small animal."

That night, the Rabbit's heart beat very fast as she hopped up to Bhaksuraka's den. She heard his stomach rumble. She took a deep breath.

"Bhaksuraka!" she called, in her loudest voice.

The huge lion walked heavily over to the tiny Rabbit. "What is this?" he said, looking over his nose. "How lucky! My dinner has come to me!"

"I have bad news," the Rabbit said. "You have always been the strongest and mightiest animal in the entire forest. But now, there is a new lion. He is even stronger and mightier than you."

"Impossible!" Bhaksuraka roared. "Take me to this new lion. I will show him who rules this forest."

The Rabbit's heart beat faster than ever. "This way!" she called.

She led Bhaksuraka through the trees. She heard his huge paws hammer the ground behind her. She heard his stomach rumble. But she reminded herself to be brave.

After a long run, they came upon a clearing in the forest. A large and deep stone well stood in the center of the clearing.

"There," the Rabbit said, nodding to the well. "Look. The lion is in there."

Bhaksuraka looked over the stone wall of the well. In the water below, he saw a powerful lion with huge teeth and enormous paws. Bhaksuraka growled and bared his teeth. The lion in the well also growled and bared his teeth. Bhaksuraka shook his wild mane. The lion in the well also shook his wild mane. Bhaksuraka roared a terrible roar. The lion in the well roared a terrible roar.

The Rabbit looked at Bhaksuraka. "I think you may have to go down there to show him who rules the forest."

"Yes!" Bhaksuraka bellowed. "I am the mightiest!" With that, he jumped into the well and landed with a splash in the water far, far below.

He shook the water out of his mane. "There is no one here!" he roared. "You tricked me!"

The Rabbit smiled just a little. "You may be mighty, but I am clever." And with that, she hopped off to tell the rest of the animals in the forest that Bhaksuraka would never bother them again. Intelligence wins over strength.

Why the Larks Flew Away

A family of four young **larks** once lived with their mother in a nest in a wheat field. At first, the nest was very safe, for it stood on the soft ground and was hidden by the wheat.

When the wheat began to ripen, the mother lark watched carefully for any sign of the coming of the reapers. She feared that the sharp knives would cut the nest and injure the young larks.

One morning, she had to leave the nest to find some breakfast for her little ones.

"Be good children and stay in the nest," she said. "If the farmer and his son pass through the field, listen very carefully to what they say."

"Yes, Mother," cried the four baby larks.

The mother lark flew away. A few minutes later, the little larks heard the farmer and his son passing along the narrow path near the nest.

---

larks a kind of songbird

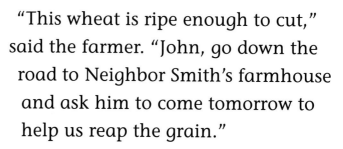

"This wheat is ripe enough to cut," said the farmer. "John, go down the road to Neighbor Smith's farmhouse and ask him to come tomorrow to help us reap the grain."

When the mother lark came home, she brought some fat worms for breakfast. She found her babies chirping excitedly.

"Mother! Mother!" they cried. "The men are coming to cut the wheat. We must move away tonight!"

"What did the farmer say?" asked the mother lark.

"The farmer told his son to go over to Neighbor Smith's house and ask him to help cut the grain."

"My dear children," laughed the mother lark, "as yet, we have nothing to fear."

When the baby larks had eaten their breakfast, the mother lark showed them how to exercise their wings.

The next morning, before leaving, the mother lark said once more, "Stay in the nest, and if the farmer passes through the field, listen to what he says."

"Yes, Mother," cried the little larks.

Away flew the mother, and again the farmer and his son passed through the fields.

"Did you ask Neighbor Smith to help us cut the grain?" inquired the farmer.

"Yes, Father," replied the son, "and I expected him here already."

"The wheat is ripe, and it should be cut without delay," replied the farmer. "**Mount** your horse and ride to your cousins' house. Ask them if they will help us."

This frightened the baby larks so much that when they saw their mother coming, they began to chirp more loudly than ever.

"What is the trouble?" called the mother as she hastened toward the nest.

"We must surely go away today!" cried the young larks. "The farmer's son has gone to bring his cousins to cut the wheat. We shall be killed if we stay here."

Again the mother laughed. "If the farmer waits for his cousins to help him, the wheat will not be cut today."

The third morning, the mother left the nest to search for food. At noon, the farmer and his son came into the field.

---

mount to get up on

WHY THE LARKS FLEW AWAY

"See how late it is," said the farmer, "and still not a man has come to help us. I see we must do the work ourselves. Let us go home and get everything ready. Tomorrow, before the sun is up, we shall begin to reap."

Soon after the farmer had gone, the mother lark came flying over the wheat field. The little larks told her all that they had heard.

"Now, indeed, it is time for us to be off," she said. "Shake your wings and get ready to fly. When a man makes up his mind to do his own work, it is sure to be done at once."

Folktales and Legends

The Stone in the Road
A Story

Early one morning, a sturdy old farmer came along the highway with his oxcart loaded with corn. "Oh, these lazy people!" he cried, driving his oxen to one side of the road. "Here is this big stone right in the middle of the road, and nobody will take the trouble to move it!" So he went on his way, scolding about the laziness of other people.

Then along came a soldier with a bright feather in his hat and a big sword at his side. He held his head high in the air and sang a merry song. Of course he did not see the stone in the road, but stumbled over it and fell flat in the dust.

When he had picked himself up, he began to scold about the country people.

"The stupid things!" he said. "Don't they know any better than to leave a stone in the road?"

An hour later, some **merchants** came down the road with their goods on pack horses, on their way to the fair.

....

merchants people who buy and sell things

When they came to the stone, they carefully drove their horses around it. "Did anyone ever see such a thing?" they said. "There is that big stone in the road, and not one man in all the country will pick it up!"

The stone lay in the road all that day until the sun began to set. Just then, a fair young milkmaid came along, singing a happy song. She nearly tripped on the stone as the soldier had! Lucky for her, she noticed it in time to stop herself. For a moment, she stood and thought. It was getting dark and she had to get home, but she worried what might happen to someone who came down the road once night had fallen.

So, with great effort, the milkmaid reached down and pulled on the edge of the stone. It only just budged, but that was enough to let her get a better grip on the rock. Then, heaving with all her might, she managed to turn the stone on its side. Finally, all by herself, she slowly pushed the heavy stone off to the side of the road. When she was finished, she clapped her hands together.

"There," the milkmaid said, "now at least no one will trip and hurt themselves."

The next morning, the entire kingdom was awakened by the sound of the king's trumpeters.

There was an announcement: every man, woman, and child was to report to the King's Highway outside the castle gates immediately. The citizens of the kingdom poured out of their homes and walked to the road. It was the very same road, of course, where the stone had sat the day before. Soon, all the people of the kingdom stood and waited there.

In the crowd stood the farmer, the soldier, the merchants, and the milkmaid. They murmured with their friends and neighbors and wondered why they'd been asked to gather that morning. They did not have to wonder for long. Soon enough the king stepped forward to address his subjects.

"I thank you all for being here this morning," the king began. "I'm sure you are curious as to why I have asked you to this spot. The reason is simple. Yesterday, a boulder sat in the middle of this road. But today, as you can see, there is no longer a stone in the road."

The members of the crowd whispered among themselves. They could see the stone on the side of the road and the marks on the road where it had been pushed. They listened as the king continued.

"Last night, the stone was moved to the side of the roadway, where it still sits. I would like the person who moved the stone to come forward."

For a long moment, no one moved. But then, at last, the milkmaid took a cautious step forward. The king looked at her and nodded.

"You moved the stone from the road?" he asked.

"Yes, sire," she replied.

"Did anyone ask you to move the stone?"

"No, sire."

"Why, then, did you move it?" the king asked.

THE STONE IN THE ROAD: A STORY

The milkmaid looked
around nervously. She
said, "I am sorry, sire. If I had
known that you wanted the stone in
the road, I never would have dreamed of moving it."

The king held up his hand, and the milkmaid
stopped talking. He repeated his question: "Why did
you move it?"

"Well, sire," the milkmaid said, "I moved it
because it was in the way. I didn't trip on it, but I
thought that someone else might."

The king nodded thoughtfully. Then he turned
to the rest of the crowd, and he spoke to them in a
booming voice.

"I placed the stone in the road yesterday as a test.
It was a test to all who came upon it. A test of who
among you would be good and decent enough to
take the trouble to move it, and thereby protect your
fellow citizens. Again and again, those of you who
encountered the stone failed the test. But this young
milkmaid passed it."

Now the crowd nodded its approval, and the
milkmaid smiled and blushed.

"And because she passed the test,"
the king continued, "she shall be
rewarded."

Now the king walked to the place
in the road where the stone previously
sat. There, he bent down, brushed away
a bit of dirt, and picked up a small
box. Standing, he opened the box and
poured into his hand a number of gold
coins. The crowd gasped at this, and the
milkmaid looked at the gold in stunned
silence.

"This," the king said as he walked over and handed the coins to the milkmaid, "is your reward for helping your fellow citizens. You protected them and did not expect somebody else to solve a problem."

The milkmaid was speechless. The gold in her hand was more wealth than she or anyone in her family had ever imagined. At last, she managed to thank the king for his generosity.

"I thank you, sire," she said quietly.

"No, young lady," the king returned. "Thank you."

The Stone in the Road
A Play

Characters

KING ALVIS, the ruler of the kingdom

SIR GAVIN THE DIM, a knight in the kingdom

FARMER

SOLDIER 1

SOLDIER 2

MILKMAID

LOYAL SUBJECTS

SETTING: *A well-worn dirt road cuts across the stage from left to right. In the far distance, a medieval castle is surrounded by a large moat. Upstage middle, a large tree stands.*

Scene 1

The curtains rise, and the stage lights come on. King Alvis pats the ground in the middle of the road. He stands just as a knight named Sir Gavin the Dim enters. Sir Gavin carries a heavy boulder, which he brings over into the middle of the road near the king.

KING ALVIS: Very good. Right here will be excellent, thank you.

Sir Gavin puts the boulder down in front of the king and, with great effort, places the stone so that it takes up the maximum amount of space and obviously blocks the path. Sir Gavin wipes his forehead and turns to the king.

SIR GAVIN: Are you sure this is what you wish, sire?

KING ALVIS: Yes, quite sure. Thank you, Sir Gavin the Dim. You may return to the castle.

Sir Gavin takes a step, but then hesitates.

SIR GAVIN: Sire? Permission to ask a question.

KING ALVIS: Permission granted. What do you wish to know, Sir Gavin?

SIR GAVIN: Well, sire…won't the boulder be in the way if it is left here? That is, won't the stone make it more difficult for people to pass on the road as they travel to and from the castle?

KING ALVIS: A fine observation, Sir Gavin. I believe that the boulder will indeed prove to be an obstacle to those who wish to pass along this road.

SIR GAVIN: And yet, your wish is that I should leave it here?

KING ALVIS: That is my wish. No doubt, you think it a strange one.

SIR GAVIN: No, sire. I just…

KING ALVIS: 'Tis perfectly understandable. It is a strange wish. Perhaps you also think it foolish.

SIR GAVIN: Sire, I do not…

KING ALVIS: Again, you may be at ease, Sir Gavin.

I admit that it certainly appears foolish. But, Sir Gavin, do you consider me to be a fool?

SIR GAVIN: Absolutely not, sire.

KING ALVIS: And my subjects—Do they commonly consider me to be a fool?

SIR GAVIN: On the contrary, sire. You are thought to be the wisest ruler our kingdom has ever known. The people sing your praises everywhere. By day, they speak of how wonderful it is to have a kind and decent king. And they rest easy at night knowing that you are here to solve their problems.

KING ALVIS: I thank you for your kind words, Sir Gavin. But you have hit upon the exact reason that I have had you place this boulder in the road.

SIR GAVIN: I'm sorry, sire. I do not understand.

KING ALVIS: Come. Hide with me behind this tree, and you shall.

The king and the knight go hide behind the tree.

Scene 2

A moment passes. Then a Farmer comes along with a wagon loaded with grain. He approaches the boulder, which blocks his path, and stops. He looks around. The king and the knight, unseen by the Farmer, poke their heads out from behind the tree to observe.

FARMER: Now, look at this! Some fool has left this stone in the middle of the road. People can be so thoughtless. Had I not noticed it, I could have crashed my cart into it and lost my entire load of grain. This stone might easily ruin the journey of anyone who uses this road. I shall have to make a report of it to the king. In the meantime, though, there is nothing to be done, I suppose.

Now the Farmer, with great difficulty, proceeds to carefully guide his wagon around the boulder in the road. Some of his grain spills, and he mutters in frustration, but he eventually makes his way around the obstacle. He then continues on his way to the castle.

KING ALVIS: Did you see what I saw, Sir Gavin?

SIR GAVIN: With my own eyes, sire.

KING ALVIS: And now do you understand why I had you place the boulder in the road?

SIR GAVIN: I'm afraid that I do not, sire.

KING ALVIS: Really?

SIR GAVIN: Apologies. Perhaps you could explain?

KING ALVIS: *(Hearing a noise)* No need. Someone else approaches. Get behind this tree with me again and watch. This time pay close attention, and you will surely understand my reasons for placing the stone in the road.

The king and Sir Gavin again hide. After a few seconds, two Soldiers come marching down the road in step. King Alvis and Sir Gavin **surreptitiously** *watch. Neither Soldier sees the boulder in the road, so one accidentally stubs his toe on it as he marches. He hops around in great pain.*

SOLDIER 1: Blast! That hurts!

SOLDIER 2: It certainly looks like it.

SOLDIER 1: Did you see that boulder?

SOLDIER 2: I did not. Did you?

....

surreptitiously   in a secret or sneaky way

SOLDIER 1: Would I have stubbed my toe on it if I had?

SOLDIER 2: I suppose not. It's not a great place for a boulder, is it?

SOLDIER 1: *(Rubbing his toe)* No! It's not! The next person who comes down this road could very easily end up doing exactly what I have done!

SOLDIER 2: That's definitely true. Too bad, isn't it?

SOLDIER 1: It is. It's a real pity.

SOLDIER 2: We should probably keep moving; are you able to walk?

SOLDIER 1: Yes, I think so. Come on. The king shall hear about this, I swear it!

The Soldiers continue to march toward the castle, exiting the stage as King Alvis and Sir Gavin again step out onto the road.

KING ALVIS: Now, after seeing that, you must at last understand why I've had you put the boulder in the road, right?

SIR GAVIN: Well…

KING ALVIS: Oh, come on. Really? Were you paying attention like I told you to?

SIR GAVIN: I was. Close attention, sire.

KING ALVIS: And you saw what happened and how the soldiers reacted?

SIR GAVIN: I did, sire.

KING ALVIS: But you still don't get it?

SIR GAVIN: I'm afraid I've never been very bright, sire.

KING ALVIS: You can say that again.

SIR GAVIN: I'm afraid I've never been…

KING ALVIS: Never mind. It's just an expression. Someone else approaches. We must hide.

The king and Sir Gavin again hide behind the tree once more.

Scene 3

The lights dim slightly; it is evening now. After a moment, a Milkmaid walks down the road. She carries pails and whistles a happy tune, but stops when she sees the boulder in front of her. She looks around. King Alvis and Sir Gavin lean out from their hiding place to watch what she does next.

MILKMAID: What's this? A stone in the road? Why, I nearly tripped on it. And now it is getting dark, and anyone else who comes down the road might also stumble or hurt themselves. I must do something about that.

The Milkmaid puts down her pails and works to move the boulder. It is not easy. She cannot lift it, so she must gradually roll it over and over until it is off the road. At last, after a great deal of effort, she manages to get the stone out of the roadway. She catches her breath, grabs her pails, and straightens up.

MILKMAID: That was difficult, but I can now rest easy knowing that I've taken care of this danger.

The Milkmaid continues on her way and exits. King Alvis and Sir Gavin step forward.

KING ALVIS: Now, at long last, do you understand why I had you place the stone in the road, Sir Gavin?

SIR GAVIN: Yes, sire.

KING ALVIS: Really?

SIR GAVIN: Um…sure…sire.

KING ALVIS: Very well. Then tell me the reason.

SIR GAVIN: Right. Okay. You had me place the boulder in the road so…that…the milkmaid could move it out of the road?

King Alvis lets out a long and deeply disappointed sigh.

KING ALVIS: *(Under his breath)* I need to find some smarter knights.

SIR GAVIN: What's that, sire?

KING ALVIS: Never you mind. I want you to go and make an announcement. The people are to meet here—on this spot—at dawn tomorrow. I have an announcement to make!

With that, Sir Gavin makes a fast exit, and King Alvis walks alone back to the castle. The lights go down.

Scene 4

*Lights up again. It is now dawn, and the Farmer, the two Soldiers, the Milkmaid, and several Loyal Subjects stand on the road near where the boulder was. They **mill about** and whisper to one another.*

SOLDIER 1: I wonder what this is about.

SOLDIER 2: I don't know. But this is where you stubbed your toe yesterday. There's the boulder.

FARMER: I nearly crashed my cart into that boulder.

More whispering among the people until, suddenly, a trumpet blast sounds and Sir Gavin steps forward.

SIR GAVIN: The honorable and good King Alvis has arrived!

Everyone bows their heads as King Alvis steps forward. He stands in the road where the boulder once sat. He clears his throat.

KING ALVIS: Thank you all for coming this morning. I have called you here for a very good reason. As many of you know, there was a boulder in the middle of this road yesterday. Indeed, the boulder sat on the very spot where I now stand.

....

mill about   to move around without purpose

But—as you can see—the stone is no longer in the road. It was moved by someone last evening. I would like the person who moved the stone to now come forward.

More whispering from the crowd. At last, the Milkmaid takes a careful step forward.

KING ALVIS: You are the one who moved the boulder, young lady?

MILKMAID: Y-Yes, sire.

KING ALVIS: Did anyone tell you to move it?

MILKMAID: No, sire.

KING ALVIS: Did anyone help you move it?

MILKMAID: No, sire.

KING ALVIS: So you alone decided to move the boulder and no one helped you—is that correct?

MILKMAID: Yes, sire.

KING ALVIS: Why did you move it, young lady?

MILKMAID: Well, sire, I moved it because it was in the way. I didn't trip on it, but I thought that someone else might.

KING ALVIS: I see. And do you know who had the boulder placed in the road, young lady?

MILKMAID: No, sire.

KING ALVIS: It was I! I had the boulder placed in the road.

More murmurs from the crowd. The Milkmaid looks left and right, obviously nervous.

KING ALVIS: And would you like to know why, young lady?

MILKMAID: Yes, sire.

KING ALVIS: It was a test. It was a test to all who came upon it. You see, for years, I have served as your king and you all have come to depend on me. You have depended on me to rule fairly, and I have tried to do so. That is acceptable. But you have also come to depend on me to solve your

problems for you. You have come to expect that I alone can help you when you face a difficult situation. That is unacceptable. So I had this boulder placed here as a test to see who in my kingdom would be able to solve a problem alone, without seeking out someone else to do it. And, this morning, I say to you all that only this young woman passed the test.

The crowd nods and whispers its approval. The Milkmaid smiles.

KING ALVIS: And because she passed the test, she shall be rewarded. Young lady, please come over to me.

The Milkmaid walks over to the king. He steps back and goes down on one knee. He brushes away a bit of dirt on the road.

KING ALVIS: It was nearly dark when you moved the boulder last night, so perhaps you did not see what was hidden under it. Or perhaps you are just too honest to take what you did not know was your prize for solving the problem on your own. But there was a box under the boulder. That box remains this morning. It is here so that the person who moved it might be rewarded for her behavior. So now, I present it to you.

The king now reaches down and pulls a small box from the ground. He hands it to the Milkmaid, who opens it. She tips it over, and out pours a handful of gold coins.

MILKMAID: Why, this is more money than my family has ever seen! Thank you! Thank you, your majesty!

KING ALVIS: No, young lady. Thank you. And may this be a lesson to all of my subjects to always work hard to solve your own problems rather than expect someone else to solve them for you.

The crowd cheers and they surround the Milkmaid to look at her gold. King Alvis moves off to the side, satisfied, and he's soon joined by Sir Gavin.

KING ALVIS: So, Sir Gavin, now you understand what I was trying to show you yesterday, yes?

SIR GAVIN: Oh, yes, sire. I understand completely. You are, as I said, very wise.

KING ALVIS: Thank you, Sir Gavin. I am glad that you've understood this lesson.

SIR GAVIN: Just one thing…I can't believe that box of gold just happened to be in the exact spot where you had me place the boulder. I mean, that's incredible. What are the chances, right? I've heard of coincidences, but this one takes the cake….

King Alvis just shakes his head as Sir Gavin the Dim continues to marvel that such a treasure would have, by chance, been found in the exact spot where the king chose to have him place the boulder.

Curtain.

The Tiger, the Brahman, and the Jackal

Once upon a time in India, a **Brahman** was walking along the road. His mind was so filled with calm thoughts that he hardly noticed where he was going.

As he walked along in peace, he was startled by the sound of a most desperate growling, roaring, and snapping of teeth.

He looked up to see a tiger caught in a large cage. The tiger was biting at the bars in rage, but in vain.

When the tiger saw the Brahman, he cried out, "My holy friend, please let me out of this trap."

The kind Brahman began to open the trap but then stopped. "No," he said, "for I fear that if I release you, you will eat me. After all, it is in your nature."

"It is in my nature to be free!" replied the tiger. "I promise, if you release me, I will do you no harm. I will serve you forever!"

Brahman a holy or wise person in Indian society

THE TIGER, THE BRAHMAN, AND THE JACKAL 49

"A Brahman has no need of a servant," said the holy man. "And besides, once you are out of this cage, you are likely to forget your promises."

The Brahman turned and began to walk away. But then the tiger called out in a pitiful voice, "Would you leave me here to die? Is that the way of a holy man?"

At this, the Brahman stopped. Then he turned back and opened the door of the cage. In one bound, the tiger popped out and grabbed the Brahman. "Thank you, my foolish friend," said the tiger. "And now, as I have been trapped for so long, and have grown very hungry, I must eat you!"

"Wait one minute!" cried the Brahman. "I gave you your freedom. Now give me a chance for mine. If I can find three things that say you should let me go free, then will you let me go?"

"I will," said the tiger, "but be quick about it. I am hungry!"

So the Brahman turned to a nearby tree and asked, "Oh, tree! You saw me let this tiger out of the trap. Is it not right that the tiger should let me go free?"

But the tree replied, "Why do you complain? Look at me. I give shade to all who pass by, and how do they thank me? They tear off my branches to feed to their animals. Take what is coming to you—be a man!"

Then the Brahman asked the same question of a buffalo. The buffalo answered, "Do you expect the tiger to thank you for what you did? Don't be foolish. Look at me. For years, as long as I gave milk, people treated me kindly and fed me well. But now that I am old, they make me pull heavy loads and feed me stale scraps. You can't expect goodness in return for goodness."

The sad Brahman asked the road what he thought of the matter. The road answered, "My good sir, do you really expect thanks for your kindness? Look at me. All day long, people walk on me. And how do they thank me for this service? They spit on me and throw their trash on me."

"Alas!" cried the Brahman. "It appears I must be eaten."

Just as the Brahman turned to face the hungry tiger, a **jackal** walked up. "Oh good and holy man," said the jackal, "why do you look so sad on such a fine day?"

The Brahman told him all that had happened. He told how he had found the tiger trapped in the cage. He told how he had let the tiger go free. He explained how he asked the tree, buffalo, and road for their opinions. "And now," he sadly concluded, "it appears I must be eaten."

The jackal scratched his head and said with a puzzled look, "Would you please tell me the story again? I'm afraid I found it very confusing."

Once more the Brahman told what had happened. When he finished, the jackal said, "I am sorry to be so **slow-witted**, but I'm afraid I still don't understand. Let me see—the tiger was walking along and found the Brahman in the cage…"

"No!" roared the tiger. "Have you no brain at all? The Brahman was not in the cage. I was in the cage!"

....

alas oh, no
jackal a kind of a wild dog found in Africa and Asia
slow-witted not smart

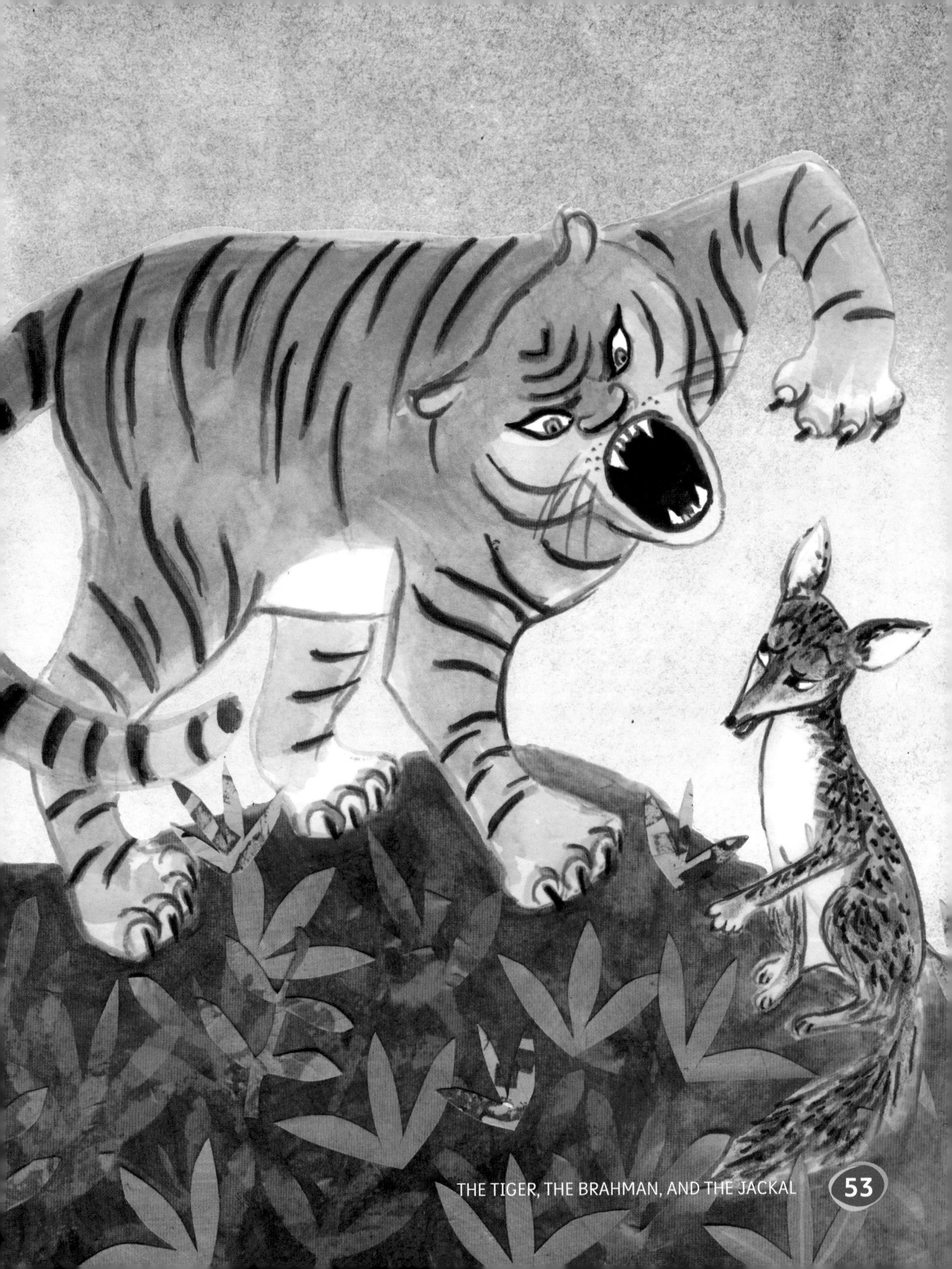

"Oh, yes, of course," said the jackal. "I was in the cage and— oh, no, that's not quite right. Let me try again. The tiger was in the Brahman, and then the buffalo opened the tiger, and—oh, dear, I'm afraid I simply can't understand it!"

"You will understand," growled the tiger. "Now listen carefully. I am the tiger. Do you see that?"

"Yes, my lord," said the jackal in a meek voice.

"And this man is the Brahman."

"Yes, my lord."

"And right here is the cage."

"Indeed, my lord."

"And I was in this cage—do you see?" said the tiger.

"Yes, my lord. I was—I mean, you were—I mean, the Brahman was—oh, dear, dear, just when it seems to make sense, I get all confused again!"

"What will it take to make you understand?" the tiger roared.

"Perhaps, my lord," said the jackal, "if we could start at the beginning, and if you would be so kind as to show me what happened. Now, the Brahman was in the cage…"

"No!" shouted the tiger. "I was in the cage—like this!" He stepped inside the cage. "Now do you understand, you foolish jackal?"

"Indeed, my lord," said the jackal as he stepped forth and, with one quick movement, shut and locked the cage. "I understand perfectly!"

Bruce and the Spider

Long ago, Robert Bruce, the king of Scotland, was hiding one day in a little hut that lay deep in the forest. He was all alone and very discouraged. He had been fighting many battles with the enemies of Scotland and had lost every battle. His soldiers had been killed or driven to take refuge in the mountains, as the king himself was now doing. He was hungry and homeless. He had no food and no place of shelter but a **mean** hut.

"There is no use in trying to free Scotland now," thought the king. "Our enemies are too strong. I might as well give up the struggle."

Just then he saw a spider trying to spin a web between two **rafters**. She would fasten one end of her thread to a rafter and then swing herself across to the other rafter. She seemed to find this very hard, for each time the thread broke, she would have to begin all over again.

---

mean run-down or poorly made
rafters beams, usually made of wood, that hold up a roof

Bruce sat watching her, and he wondered how long she would keep trying before she gave up. Six times the spider tried to fasten her thread, and six times she failed.

"You are a brave and patient spider," thought the king. "You do not give up as soon as I do. I will watch you try the seventh time. If you succeed, I too will risk my seventh battle."

Once more the spider swung her tiny thread to the opposite rafter, and this time it held fast.

"You have taught me a lesson, little spider," said Bruce. "I will gather my army and try once more to drive away the enemies of Scotland."

So the king stood again at the head of his army, and he fought as he had never fought before. This time, he won the battle and made his country free.

Myths

Tangled Webs
The Story of Arachne

In the city of Athens in the days of long ago, there lived a **maiden** named Arachne.

Arachne was skilled in the art of spinning and weaving. Not one of the maidens of Athens could spin such fine thread or weave such wonderful cloth as she could.

As time went on, Arachne grew vain and proud. "I am the most wonderful spinner and weaver in the world," she said.

"Next to our great goddess Athena," added the good people of Athens.

"Nay," said Arachne boldly, "I do not fear even Athena's skill and power. I know that I can spin and weave as well as she."

"Take care," said the wise people of Athens. "Take care, for your boasting may anger Athena."

Still Arachne did not heed their warning. She grew more vain and boasted more and more.

....

maiden a young woman who is not married

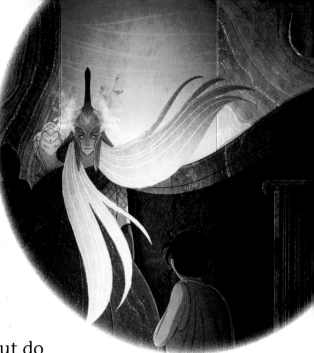

At last the goddess took notice of her foolish boasting.

One day as Arachne was working at her **loom**, an old woman appeared before her.

"My dear," said the stranger, "you boast that you are as skillful as Athena. Try your skill with the maidens, but do not **strive** with the goddess."

"I am not afraid of Athena," said the maiden. "Let her try her skill with me if she dares."

Then the stranger threw back her dark cloak and showed herself—the beautiful, golden-haired, gray-eyed Athena. "I am ready," she said.

The other maidens were frightened. Only Arachne was not afraid. "Let us begin," she said.

"First, hear this," said Athena. "If your cloth is best, I will weave no more. But if mine is best, you will never weave again. Do you agree?"

"I agree," said Arachne.

....

loom a frame or machine used for weaving cloth
strive to try very hard; to struggle

TANGLED WEBS: THE STORY OF ARACHNE

Then the people of Athens looked on in wonder as the goddess and the maiden worked at their looms.

Athena wove into her cloth pictures of the great gods—Zeus and Hera, Apollo and Poseidon, and all the others. No one had ever seen anything as wonderful as her pictures.

Arachne had great skill, but the pictures that she wove were not noble and beautiful like Athena's. They showed her own proud spirit.

As soon as her cloth was finished, Arachne looked at the other cloth. She knew that it was much more beautiful than hers. She was filled with grief and anger. "If I can never weave again, how can I live? All my joy in life is gone. Let me die."

"Nay," said Athena, "you shall not die. You shall go on spinning and weaving forever." And with a touch, she turned Arachne into the first spider, which ran to a corner and quickly wove a beautiful, shining web.

"You and your kind," said Athena, "shall always be the greatest spinners and weavers on the earth."

Repeat After Me, Me, Me...
The Story of Echo

Long ago in ancient Greece, there lived a **nymph** named Echo. Like many nymphs, Echo was beautiful. She had long dark hair and dark brown eyes. Also, like many nymphs, Echo loved music. She could often be heard singing by a mountain stream or dancing along a woodland trail.

Yes, Echo was similar to other nymphs in many ways. But one thing made Echo different. One thing made her stand out. Unlike other nymphs, what Echo most enjoyed was talking.

For, you see, Echo was quite smart and very funny. She could chat for long stretches of time about any subject in the world. And she was never at a loss for words. She was always ready with a clever remark or a smart observation. It was said that there was no better way to pass an hour than in conversation with Echo.

---

nymph in mythology, one of the minor goddesses of nature represented as beautiful maidens living in mountains, forests, meadows, and waters

So it is not surprising that those who spent time with Echo always enjoyed her company.

Now, Echo's home was on a mountain in the middle of Greece. Yet, over time, Echo's **reputation** spread. Men and women and gods and goddesses in all places knew her name and heard about her intelligence and wit. Eventually, word of Echo even reached the home of the Greek gods, Mount Olympus. There, her fame attracted the attention of Zeus, the king of the gods.

Zeus listened to the stories about Echo. He heard about her gift with language—how much everyone loved to speak with her—and his interest grew. At last, he decided that he had to meet Echo himself. So one morning, before the sun rose, he left Mount Olympus.

Zeus traveled hundreds of miles to reach the mountain where Echo lived. He found her at home.

---

reputation seen by others to have some quality or ability; fame

He introduced himself. He told her that he had come a long way to see her. And he asked Echo to take a walk with him.

Echo agreed.

For hours, Zeus and Echo chatted. They spoke about her home and about his. They talked about the animals who lived on the mountain and the people whose village sat in its shadow. And the longer they spoke, the more charmed by Echo Zeus became. Yes, she was beautiful, but it was Echo's sparkling conversation that truly captured Zeus.

"I wonder," Zeus said, "if you might consider leaving your home."

"But I have left it," Echo replied with a wink. "Did you not realize that we are outside? Indeed, we've been walking along this trail for hours."

Zeus smiled. "You are very clever. I will have to be clearer. I wonder if you might leave here and return with me to Mount Olympus. You would be very welcome there. And then I won't have to travel so far every time I wish to talk with you."

"I wonder," Echo said, "whether Hera would welcome me to Mount Olympus."

Zeus nodded at that, for he well knew how jealous his wife could be. But what he did not know was that Hera had followed him that day. He did not know that she had been watching him and Echo all along. He did not know that, even now, his wife was listening from behind a nearby tree as he spoke to Echo.

Which is why Zeus was so shocked when, at that moment, Hera stormed out from the woods. The king of the gods was speechless, and Hera's eyes glowed with a jealous fire. She stood before her husband and Echo on the mountain path.

"You dare to betray me like this?" Hera said to Zeus. "You dare to invite this creature to our home? I shall never allow it!"

"Hera!" Zeus shouted. "Calm yourself!"

"Calm myself?" Hera returned just as loudly. "You have secretly left our home. You have traveled halfway across Greece. You have spent hours with Echo. And you have done it all behind my back. Why in the world should I be calm?"

"Well," Echo said in relaxed tones, "for one thing, all of your yelling is scaring the birds."

She meant it as a joke. She hoped it might ease some of the **tension** of the moment. She did not mean to insult Hera.

Yet Hera was insulted. She glared at Echo. She fumed. She decided then and there to punish this nymph whom everyone thought was so clever. So that's when Hera put a curse on Echo.

"Clever thing," Hera said coldly. "You're the nymph who always knows what to say. You can turn a phrase like no one else. That's what everyone says, right?"

"Please," Echo began, "I didn't mean to offend you. I'm sorry. I—"

"Silence!" Hera interrupted. "I think I've heard enough of your witty talk. So from this day on, you shall no longer be able to say anything original!

....

tension a feeling of nervousness or fear that makes it hard to relax

All you will be able to do is repeat others. Every word out of your mouth shall be the exact words that another just spoke."

"No, please," Echo whimpered.

"Hera, don't!" Zeus said.

But Hera ignored their begging. She continued venomously: "This shall be your curse, Echo!"

And when Echo tried to object again, when she tried to argue more, these were the only words she was able to produce: "Curse, Echo!"

Zeus's eyes fell. He looked at Hera, who glared at him. There was nothing he could do. He reached out to touch Echo's hand.

"I'm sorry, Echo," he said. "Good-bye."

And all Echo could do was repeat him: "Good-bye."

That is why, today, when you are in the mountains and you yell something out and hear your words repeated back to you, it's known as an echo.

A Flight Through the Sky
The Story of Daedalus

Long ago on a faraway island, there lived a man named Daedalus.

Daedalus was famed throughout the land for his skill with his hands. No other man of his time was so clever in building. His mind was always full of plans to make something new.

But though he was held in great honor, Daedalus was really a prisoner. The cruel king of the island knew how skillful he was and would not let him go away.

As time went on, Daedalus grew weary of his life on the island and wished to escape. But it was impossible for him to get away by sea. On every side, the king's strong ships kept watch.

For a long time, Daedalus wondered how he could escape. At last he hit upon a daring plan.

"The king may control the land and sea," he said, "but he does not control the air. I will go that way."

No man had ever before tried to do what he
planned to do. He planned to make two sets of wings,
one for himself and one for his young son Icarus, so
that they could fly away.

He set to work secretly collecting feathers, small
ones and large ones. Then he made a light frame of
wood, with cloth stretched over it. Very carefully he
laid the feathers all over the frame, and held them
firmly in place with wax.

Night after night he worked in secret, until at last
he had finished a pair of wings. As soon as these
were ready, he strapped them on his son's shoulders.
He showed the boy how to flap them like a bird, and
slowly young Icarus learned to fly.

Each night Daedalus secretly worked on the second pair of wings, and each night Icarus tried his skill at flying.

At last all was ready. Early in the morning, Daedalus and his son stole down to the beach, carrying their wings.

As the father strapped the boy's wings in place, he said, "Icarus, my son, listen to what I say. Be sure to keep the middle track. If you fly too low over the sea, your wings will get wet. If you go too high, the heat of the sun will melt the wax on your wings. Be very careful. Do not fly too close to the sun."

Icarus promised, eager to be off. Then as Daedalus gave the word, they raised their wings and rose up, up over the sea like great birds.

The morning sun shone on their feathers so that they glistened like gold. The cool air from the ocean touched their faces. A great thrill went through the boy as he felt himself soaring up through the morning air.

He forgot his father's warning. He swooped down to the waves, and then rose again higher and higher into the sky.

Suddenly, before he could stop himself, he had flown too near the hot sun. The burning heat melted the wax. The feathers loosened and fell in a soft shower into the water.

In vain Icarus flapped his arms. His wings were now useless. Down he dropped—down, down to the sea.

"Icarus," cried his father. "Icarus, where are you?" No answer came. Only the feathers floating on the water showed him what had happened.

Poor Daedalus flew on till he came safely to land. But he was so sad at the loss of his son that he never used his wings again.

Roll, Roll, Roll That Rock
The Story of Sisyphus

Long ago in the south of Greece, there lived a king. His name was Sisyphus. He was a famous king. He was a powerful king. But he was not always a good king.

Sisyphus often acted selfishly. He treated others poorly. He could be cruel and coldhearted. Worst of all, Sisyphus was overly proud.

"I'm the king," he **proclaimed**. "I rule over everyone and everything. I can do whatever I want because no one has the power to punish me!"

One day, a friend tried to remind Sisyphus that the gods were more powerful than he.

"Your highness," the friend said. "I think that, maybe, Apollo is more powerful than you."

"Apollo? The god of the sun? He is not as powerful as me," Sisyphus replied.

"What about Ares, god of war?" the friend asked.

"Ares is weak compared to me," Sisyphus declared.

---

proclaimed announced or claimed strongly

"Zeus then," the friend offered. "Zeus is the king of the gods. He is the most powerful of them all."

Still, Sisyphus scoffed.

"Zeus is a fool!" he said. "I will prove that neither Apollo nor Ares nor Zeus is more powerful than me."

Then Sisyphus looked to the sky. He stretched his arms out wide. He spoke in a loud booming voice.

"Gods," Sisyphus said. "I am more powerful than any of you! And if I am wrong, then punish me for saying so! Please, I welcome your punishment!"

Then he waited and waited and waited. But nothing happened. So Sisyphus felt very clever, and he went on believing that he was more powerful than the gods and had no need to fear them.

A few weeks later, Sisyphus was walking on the beach. Over the sound of the waves, he heard a noise. It sounded like someone yelling. Sisyphus looked up to see a giant bird flying across the sky.

The bird held a nymph in its talons. The nymph's name was Aegina. She was the daughter of the river god, Asopus. Sisyphus recognized her at once.

"Help me!" Aegina cried out.

Of course, Sisyphus could not reach Aegina to help her. But he did watch where the giant bird took her. He saw the bird and Aegina land on an island called Oenone that was west of his kingdom.

Soon after, a visitor came to Sisyphus's palace. The visitor was Asopus, Aegina's father. He was searching for his daughter, and he thought perhaps Sisyphus could help.

"Zeus turned himself into a giant bird," Asopus told Sisyphus. "Then he swooped down and grabbed my daughter in his talons. I saw him fly off toward your kingdom. Have you seen her?"

Sisyphus looked at Asopus. He was a god, and yet he needed Sisyphus's help. This only confirmed Sisyphus's belief that he was more powerful than the gods. He came up with what he thought was a very clever plan.

Sisyphus replied, "Perhaps I have seen your daughter, and perhaps I have not. Perhaps I would be willing to tell you what I know. Perhaps not. But first, you must do something for me."

"Anything," Asopus cried. "I'll do anything to learn where my daughter is."

"Very good," Sisyphus said. "Now listen to me, Asopus. You are the god of rivers, and my kingdom has several rivers in it."

"This is true," said Asopus.

"Yet I must have servants fetch water from a river whenever I want a drink and whenever I want a bath."

"Of course," said Asopus.

"Well, I'm tired of having to wait for my water to be brought to me," Sisyphus said.

"I see," said Asopus.

"So," Sisyphus continued, "I want you to make a freshwater spring appear in my palace. Then I can have my water right away at all times. Do that, and I will tell you what I have seen."

Asopus quickly agreed. At that very moment, in the courtyard of the royal palace, a natural spring bubbled up from the ground. Just like that, the king had all the fresh water he could want right in his own home. He smiled at Asopus.

"I saw your daughter being carried to the island of Oenone," he said. "I would bet that she is still there. For Zeus is a fool, and he has no idea that I saw him take Aegina there."

Asopus knew the island of Oenone. He left to travel there immediately. And when he arrived, he tried to rescue his daughter from Zeus.

Zeus was shocked to see Asopus. He hurled lightning bolts at him. He refused to return Aegina. He sent Asopus away from Oenone, but first he demanded that Asopus reveal how he learned their **whereabouts**. When Asopus told Zeus the story, Zeus grew furious.

....

whereabouts place or location where a person or thing is

"Sisyphus is a mortal king!" Zeus yelled. "How dare he call me a fool and meddle in the affairs of the gods!"

Then and there, Zeus decided to punish Sisyphus. He came up with a curse. And he swore that the mortal king would learn just how powerful and clever the king of the gods actually was.

First, Zeus banished Sisyphus to the underworld. There, he demanded that Sisyphus complete one task: push a large boulder up a hill.

Now, the boulder was heavy. The hill was high. Yet Sisyphus believed that once the boulder reached the top of the hill, he would be free. So he set to pushing the boulder.

But there was something Sisyphus did not know. Zeus had put a spell on the boulder. Zeus made it so the boulder would magically roll back down the hill as soon as it neared the top.

Thus Sisyphus's task would never end. He would be doomed to push that boulder up that hill for all time. He would be eternally frustrated. He would be forever punished for believing himself to be more powerful and clever than the gods.

And this is why today, difficult and frustrating tasks that never seem to end are often called *Sisyphean*.

What Do You Think?

Bury All Utility Wires

Everyone has seen them. We pass them every day. They stand next to our homes. They are outside our offices. They are tall. They are ugly. And they're just waiting to cause problems. They are the large **utility poles** that dot our streets. They hold up our power lines and our telephone wires.

But do they have to? Must they always be there? Can we somehow get rid of these big ugly poles for good?

Of course, we can. Of course, we should. Of course, we must.

And here's the good news: It's pretty simple. We can bury all utility wires underground. Doing so will remove these eyesores from our city and make life better for residents.

Burying utility wires will protect them. They will no longer be at the mercy of the weather. That's good news for everyone. It means no more **power outages** when summer storms hit. Internet and television

---

utility poles tall poles that support wiring that connects utilities— telephone, electrical, and other services—to their customers

power outages loss of electricity for some period of time

service won't be disrupted when winter ice freezes the cables overhead. Phone lines will never again go down like they did during last fall's hurricane.

These outages bother everybody. Now, we can make them a thing of the past. Putting the wires underground will ensure consistent service. For that reason alone, it is a slam dunk.

But it's not just about protecting the wires. It's also about protecting people and animals.

We all recall when Foster Street was shut down because of a downed wire in July. It nearly started a fire. The Independence Day parade had to be rerouted. No one has forgotten Mayor Greene's car accident in January. Her van slid on ice and smashed into a utility pole. The whole city feared the worst. Everyone remembers when a damaged wire electrocuted an eagle last April. We all felt so sad. That poor bird never had a chance.

If we bury all utility wires, these dangers will disappear. These incidents will no longer occur. Once buried, no live wires can fall to the ground and endanger us. There will be no more poles for cars to crash into. We'll never again

have to fear that wildlife will be injured. Again, as far as safety goes, this idea is a home run.

Still not convinced? There's more.

Once we bury our utility wires, we can take down those ugly poles. Our **landscape** will be free of them forever. The poles will no longer stand out on our lovely tree-lined streets. They will not interrupt the views of our beautiful countryside. Our city will look as it did when it was founded 150 years ago. It will, once again, be as pretty as a postcard.

Now, of course there will be **objections**. That's no surprise. People will complain about the idea.

....

landscape everything you can see when you look across an area of land
objections reasons or arguments against, or opposed to, something

They'll **nitpick**. They'll invent problems. This is all **predictable**.

Some will say that burying the wires will take too long. Others will insist that taking down the poles will cost too much. Still others will swear that there are better ways to spend the city's money.

But they are wrong.

Burying the wires will not take long at all. The project can be completed in a matter of months. Once trenches are dug, it's simply a matter of having crews lay down the wires. Truly, the work will be over before most people even notice it has begun.

....

nitpick to engage in fussy criticism over small details
predictable known or understood to be likely to happen

Further, it will hardly cost anything. The city will have to pay the workers to bury the lines. It will have to buy or rent some equipment. It will have to cover the cost of taking down the poles. These are small expenses. In fact, burying wires actually saves money in the long run.

Why? Because we will never again have to repair poles. We will no longer have to replace wires damaged by weather. Maintenance costs will almost disappear. Yes, we may spend a lot of money now. But we will save even more later.

Lastly, there is no better way to spend this money. This is a project that has no downside. Think about that. It's not something you can say for other public projects.

You want to repair the library? Okay, but not everyone uses the library. You want to repave I-76? Fine, but plenty of folks don't take I-76; they drive on Route 522 instead. You think we should fix up the Oak Lane Playground? Well, people without kids never go to that playground.

Do you see the difference?

Everyone has a refrigerator. Everyone uses the phone. Everyone relies on utility wires. So burying them will make life easier, safer, and more pleasant for everyone. Further, it will not make life worse for anyone. No one will suffer because of this project. Honestly, good luck finding a better way to spend the money.

Utility poles are everywhere. They are on busy city streets. They are on quiet country roads. Maybe there was a time when they were necessary. Perhaps there was a moment when wires had to be above ground. It's even possible that people once liked how utility poles looked.

But that time is over. That moment has passed.

Today, the best place for utility wires is out of sight. They belong underground. Burying them will improve service. It will reduce danger. And it will make our city more attractive.

We can do it. We must do it. We will do it.

Keep Our Wires High in the Sky

People are talking about it. Reporters are writing about it. **Politicians** are making promises about it. Suddenly, everyone in town seems to have an interest in one topic. So what is that topic?

Is it the state of our roads? Is it the latest increase in local taxes? Is it the closing of the car factory on Route 9?

Nope. It's the idea that we should tear down every utility pole in town and bury our wires underground.

....

politicians people active in government, usually from getting elected to office

This **proposal**'s supporters swear it will make life better. They promise it will make people safer. They insist it will beautify our town.

But the truth is that burying utility wires is a silly idea. It's a waste of time and money. And it won't do any of the things these folks say it will do. Indeed, it will just lead to more problems. The wires, and the poles that hold them up, should stay right where they are.

The first thing people who want to bury the wires say is that it will improve service. They claim it will prevent power outages. It will keep phone and cable service from being **disrupted**. This simply isn't true. Outages are a fact of life. Disruptions will happen. This is true no matter where the wires are placed.

Sure, utility wires will not come down during thunderstorms if they are buried. But what will happen when animals dig them up? Or when tree roots grow into and through them? Or when there is a flood? What will happen when construction crews accidentally **sever** the wires as they dig foundations for new buildings?

....

proposal a suggestion or offer given for consideration
disrupted caused disorder or interrupted the normal course of things
sever to cut, divide, or become separated

It's clear what will happen: outages. Burying wires will only make them harder to repair. Because it won't just be a matter of being lifted up by a truck to fix the problem. No. Instead, crews will have to close roads and dig up the ground before they can get to work.

Does that sound more convenient to anyone?

Another favorite argument of those who want to bury wires is that it is safer. They point out that downed wires are dangerous. They mention that cars occasionally crash into utility poles. Once the wires are buried and the poles gone, they say, these things won't happen.

KEEP OUR WIRES HIGH IN THE SKY

Give me a break.

Of course, downed wires are a threat. And, yes, it's bad when a car slides on ice and rams a utility pole. But do you know what an even bigger threat is? Do you know what's worse than hitting a pole? When a kid digging a hole strikes one of the buried wires. Or when that car slides past where a utility pole would have been and smashes into a storefront. Or it hits a family on the sidewalk. The idea that burying utility wires is safer than stringing them between poles is nuts.

Then there's the idea that utility poles are ugly. There are people who think burying wires and removing poles will make the city look better. This is a weak position.

Whether something is **attractive** or not is a matter of opinion. Some people may like the way utility poles look. Others may not even notice that they are there. There are almost **definitely** some people in town who think the water tower on Hot Springs Road is ugly. Should we bury that, too?

Those who want to bury our wires aren't always honest about the project, either. They say it will be quick.

---

attractive appealing or pleasing in appearance
definitely certainly; clearly; without a doubt

They claim it will be cheap. They promise it will help everyone.

So will it?

First of all, it will not be quick. There are hundreds of miles of utility wires in the city. Trenches for each one must be dug. Then the wires have to be moved and buried. Then the poles must be taken down. Don't believe anyone who says this will be a quick job. It will take more than a year.

Second, it won't be cheap. The men and women who do the work must be paid. The city will have to buy or rent the **equipment**. And what happens when a worker accidentally strikes a water pipe? What happens when a trench needs to be dug on private property? Delays and problems will occur, and they will further drive up the cost.

Third, the project won't help everyone. Currently, the city employs dozens of people whose job is to repair wires and poles. What happens to their jobs after this project is complete? Some of them—maybe most of them—will be out of work. It doesn't sound like the project helps them, does it?

....

equipment tools, gear, or supplies needed for a purpose

Burying utility wires is just an idea right now. It's something people are thinking about. It's something people are discussing. It should not be something that we do.

Burying wires will not improve service. It will not improve safety. It will not make the town prettier. It will simply take a lot of time, cost a lot of money, and lead to the loss of several jobs. Let's allow the utility wires and the poles to stay right where they are.

Down with Fast Food

Every day, millions of people eat fast food. They order burgers and French fries. They down chicken fingers and hoagies. They guzzle sodas and milkshakes. Why? Well, one reason is that fast food is convenient. Another is that fast food is cheap. And a third reason is that they like the way fast food tastes. But I want to make one thing very clear: Each and every person who chooses to eat fast food is making a mistake. I don't think anyone should ever—EVER—eat fast food.

Let me begin with the most important reason to avoid fast food: It is terribly unhealthy. Fast food burgers and pizzas are loaded with fat. French fries and fried chicken come with tons of salt. The drinks people **swill** to wash down fast food are swimming with sugar. These are facts, and they make it clear that eating fast food is a recipe for getting heart disease. It's

....

swill to drink greedily; to guzzle

a **formula** for developing high blood pressure. It's a fool-proof plan for ending up with **diabetes**.

These facts would be bad enough. But it gets much worse.

For fast food is also **addictive**. People don't eat fast food, realize it's awful, and never have it again. Rather, they get hooked on these fatty, salty, sugary meals. They begin to **crave** them. They eat them more and more. Before long, fast food can go from something one eats now and then to a regular part of one's diet. In other words, fast food can become a habit.

It is not at all difficult to understand why that's a problem. Nevertheless, I will spell it out. The more fast food a person eats, the less healthy he or she becomes. And the longer one eats fast food, the harder it is to reverse course and undo the damage it causes. In my view, no food—no matter how tasty it is—is worth risking one's well-being to enjoy. The best way to avoid the long-term risks of eating fast food is to never start eating it in the first place.

....

formula a recipe, method, or way to make something happen
diabetes serious disease in which the body cannot properly control its blood sugar level
addictive habit-forming, causing dependence
crave to yearn for or want greatly

So, okay, protecting one's health is one big reason to **shun** fast food. That should probably be enough. But if it isn't, there are plenty of other reasons to ditch it. For instance, fast food also tastes pretty bad.

Now, I know that sounds strange. If fast food tastes bad, why do so many people eat it? Well, it all goes back to what people are really tasting when they eat fast food. It's not the meat or the potatoes that taste good to people; it's the fat and the salt that the fast food versions of those things contain.

Fast food chains use low-quality meat that they fry to mask its flavor. Their vegetables are cooked in oil or butter and robbed of their **nutrients**. They soak their noodles in sauces. Even their salads come drowning in sickeningly rich dressings. As a result, fast food dishes do not taste anything like what the same thing would taste like at home.

Compare a fast food burger to a burger grilled in the backyard. Compare greasy chicken served in a cheap cardboard bucket to fresh organic chicken baked in one's own kitchen. What will quickly become clear is

shun to avoid purposely; to avoid by habit
nutrients those things that plants, animals, and people need to live and grow

that homemade food tastes much, much better. Why? Because it is fresh. Because it is not loaded with fillers. Because it is not cooked in a way that hides the true taste of the dish.

Of course, a major argument people make in support of fast food is that it is cheap. They point out that, for example, it's possible to feed a family of four at a fast food restaurant for under $20. To that argument I say, big deal.

It's possible to feed a family of four at home for far less than $20. And one doesn't have to endanger his or her health in the process. The claim that fast food is the cheapest thing available is a myth.

Think about this. I went to the grocery store last weekend. I spent about $6 on a pound of lean ground beef. Two chicken breasts cost me $8. I bought a large bag of string beans for $2. And a big container of brown rice set me back about the same.

I took those four items home, and I prepared a meal using them and a few spices and herbs already in my kitchen. Nothing was coated in butter. Nothing was fried. Yet it turned out to be a real feast. I served six people, and there were leftovers. The total cost of the meal was about $18.

So let's review. The food I made at home was healthier than fast food. It was fresher than fast food. It tasted better than fast food. And it cost less than fast food. Sure, I had to take an hour or so to make it. But, to me, spending an hour to ensure that the people I care about had a nutritious, wholesome meal was well worth it.

As we ate the meal I made, I looked around the dining room table. I saw everyone enjoying themselves, and I thought about folks who eat a lot of fast food. I thought about what they are missing. I thought about the damage they are doing to themselves.

I realized that many people do not understand how dangerous fast food really is. Many think it is their only option. And while it made me feel sad, it also made me want to act. I felt the urge to share the truth about fast food. I wanted to let people know that they have choices. I wanted to tell them that there are healthier, tastier, and cheaper ways to eat. All they have to do is put down the fast food, and try something better.

In Favor of Fast Food

A lot of people have thoughts about fast food. Most people are against it. They say it's unhealthy. They say it tastes bad. They say it can't compete with food that is homemade. Well, I'm here to say these folks are wrong. I'm here to announce that there's nothing wrong with eating fast food. More than that, I'm here to declare that I'm in favor of fast food.

Now, the first argument most people make when they dismiss fast food is that it isn't good for you. They rant about how much fat there is in a hamburger or an order of French fries. They rave about the amount of salt in a hoagie. They get all worked up about sugary sodas.

You know what, though? They can lose their cool all they like.

I want to stay calm. I want to be **logical**. So logic forces me to admit that burgers and fries are not healthy. Obviously, hot dogs and sodas are not good for you. But logic also makes me state that,

---

logical reasonable or sensible

when it comes to fast food today, these are not the
only options out there.

There are dozens of healthy fast food choices.
There are fast food chains that just sell salads. There
are fast food places devoted to sushi. There's even a
fast food restaurant near my house that only offers
vegan dishes. These kinds of food are usually thought
of as quite healthy. So are they suddenly bad for you
when they're served as fast food?

Of course not. A salad from a fast food restaurant
is just as healthy as a salad from a **trendy bistro** or
an elegant inn. Those who insist that all fast food is
unhealthy are simply painting with too broad a brush.

----

vegan including nothing of animal origin
trendy currently fashionable
bistro a small, casual restaurant

It's time for them to be **rational** and logical. It's time for them to recognize that there are many types of fast food. And not all types are fatty, salty, and sugary.

Another favorite argument against fast food is that it tastes bad. Well, obviously, whether something tastes good or bad is a matter of opinion. There are lots of fast food restaurants whose food I do not like. There are sandwich joints with bland bread. There are pizza shops where the cheese is rubbery. There's one famous fast food chain whose chicken is always as dry as a bone. But—and I'm not a lawyer—I don't think that there is any law that says I must eat at any of these fast food restaurants.

I live near a large mall. The mall has a food court. I went there last weekend, and I counted how many

rational able to reason; reasonable

restaurants there are in the food court. I tallied 25. And at every single one of them, there was a line in front of the register. Each line had at least four people in it.

So what does that tell me? Does it tell me that more than 100 people are lining up to eat food they hate?

Again, of course not. It tells me that more than 100 people in that mall enjoyed the food served by the restaurant they lined up in front of. Every one of those people could have eaten at one of 24 other restaurants. They had choices. They weren't eating fast food because they had to. They were eating fast food because they wanted to. They were eating fast food because they like the way it tastes.

Finally, there is the argument that homemade food is better than fast food. And, look, I understand that **position**. Nobody loves their grandmother's meatballs more than me. Nobody is more excited than I am when Dad makes his famous sweet potatoes.

The thing is, though, these dishes take time. Grandma doesn't just whip up her meatballs in 10 minutes. Dad can't roast his sweet potatoes in the time it takes to go through the drive through. Homemade food is great, but homemade food is slow.

....

position a stand or opinion about a topic or issue

In a world where everyone is rushing to soccer practice and piano lessons, there just isn't always time for slow food.

Fast food solves this problem. It makes life easier. People don't have to worry about blocking off hours a day to cook. Instead, they can make a quick stop at a restaurant. They can get themselves tasty food right away. It might not be Grandma's meatballs or Dad's sweet potatoes, but it's still yummy. More importantly, it's **convenient**. It lets people continue to lead their busy, fulfilling lives.

Fast food is here to stay. People can object to it, but it isn't going to go away. I'm glad about that. There are so many great kinds of fast food. Lots of it is healthy. Much of it is tasty. All of it is convenient. And there's nothing wrong with that.

....

convenient handy, easy to get to, or nearby

Weather, Weather Everywhere

April Rain Song

by Langston Hughes

Let the rain kiss you.
Let the rain beat upon your head with silver liquid drops.
Let the rain sing you a **lullaby**.

lullaby a song meant to help a child fall asleep

The rain makes still pools on the sidewalk.
The rain makes running pools in the gutter.
The rain plays a little sleep-song on our roof at night—

And I love the rain.

The Raindrops' Ride

Some little drops of water
Whose home was in the sea,
To go upon a journey
Once happened to agree.

A white cloud was their carriage;
Their horse, a playful breeze;
And over town and country
They rode along at ease.

But oh! there were so many,
At last the carriage broke,
And to the ground came tumbling
Those frightened little folk.

Among the grass and flowers
They then were forced to roam,
Until a **brooklet** found them
And carried them all home.

....

brooklet a small brook

The Building of the Nest

by Margaret E. Sangster

They'll come again to the apple tree—
Robin and all the rest—
When the orchard branches are fair to see,
In the snow of the blossom dressed;
And the prettiest thing in the world will be
The building of the nest.

Weaving it well, so round and trim,
Hollowing it with care,
Nothing too far away for him,
Nothing for her too fair,
Hanging it safe on the topmost limb,
Their castle in the air.

Ah! mother bird, you'll have weary days
When the eggs are under your breast,
And shadow may darken the dancing rays
When the wee ones leave the nest;

But they'll find their wings in a glad **amaze**,
And God will see to the rest.

So come to the trees with all your train
When the apple blossoms blow;
Through the April shimmer of sun and rain,
Go flying **to and fro**;
And sing to our hearts as we watch again
Your fairy building grow.

....

amaze an old-fashioned word for "a surprise"
to and fro back and forth

The Secret

We have a secret, just we three,
The robin, and I, and the sweet cherry tree;
The bird told the tree, and the tree told me,
And nobody knows it but just we three.

But of course the robin knows it best,
Because she built the—I shan't tell the rest;
And laid the four little—something in it—
I'm afraid I shall tell it every minute.

But if the tree and the robin don't peep,
I'll try my best the secret to keep;
Though I know when the little birds fly about
Then the whole secret will be out.

First Snow

by Marie Louise Allen

Snow makes whiteness where it falls.
The bushes look like popcorn-balls.
And places where I always play,
Look like somewhere else today.

Winter Jewels

by Mary F. Butts

A million little diamonds
Twinkled on the trees,
And all the little maidens said,
"A jewel, if you please!"
But while they held their hands outstretched,
To catch the diamonds gay,
A million little sunbeams came
And stole them all away.

Lessons Learned

Squirrel and Spider

Once Squirrel wanted to grow a crop of grain on his farm. He worked hard to get his farm in fine condition. He dug the soil, planted and watered the seeds, and pulled the weeds. Day after day he worked, and at night he went home to his tree to rest. Since Squirrel was very good at climbing trees, he did not need to make a road to his farm. Instead he traveled to and from his farm by jumping from one tree to another.

One day, when Squirrel's grain was almost ripe, Spider went out looking for food. Along the way, Spider came near Squirrel's farm. In the distance, he could see the tall grain waving in the breeze.

"What fine-looking fields," Spider thought greedily. "I would be very pleased to have fields like these, and all that grain for myself."

Spider searched for a road to the farm, but he could not find one since Squirrel reached the farm by jumping from tree to tree. Spider went home. He told his family all about the fine farm he had found. Then cunning Spider made a plan.

The very next day, the whole Spider family started out early. Spider and his wife and children worked together all day to build a road to the farm.

When they finished making the road, Spider built his web across it. Then he threw pieces of clay pots along the path. He made it look like his children had dropped the pieces while working on the farm.

Spider's trickery made it look like the farm belonged to him. Now he and his family began to cut down Squirrel's good, ripe grain and carry it away.

Squirrel saw that someone was robbing his fields. At first he did not know who could be stealing his grain.

He said to himself, "I will watch for the thief." So he hid in a tall tree nearby.

Soon enough, Spider came to the fields again to take more grain. Squirrel jumped out of his tree.

"What right do you have to take my grain?" Squirrel asked Spider. But Spider at once asked him the very same question.

"What right do you have to take my grain?" demanded Spider.

"These are my fields," said Squirrel.

"Oh, no! They are mine," replied Spider.

"I dug them and planted them and watered them and weeded them," said Squirrel.

"Then where is your road to them?" asked crafty Spider.

"I need no road. I travel by the trees," said Squirrel. Spider laughed at such an answer. He continued to use the farm as if it were his own.

Squirrel went to a judge to say whose farm it was.

The judge scratched his chin and thought. Then he said, "No one has ever had a farm without a road leading to it. So the land must belong to Spider."

Poor Squirrel tried to explain, but the judge would allow no argument. In much joy, Spider and his family gathered all the rest of the grain from the farm. They cut it and tied it in large bundles. Then they started for the nearest market to sell it.

When they were about halfway to the market, a storm overtook them. Spider and his family ran for shelter. But the winds were so strong that they could not carry their bundles with them. They had to leave the bundles of grain by the side of the road.

When the storm was over, Spider and his family returned to pick up their grain. As they approached the spot where they had left it, they saw a large black crow.

His broad wings were stretched over the bundles to keep them dry. Spider approached Crow.

"Thank you for so kindly taking care of my grain," said Spider. Then he tried to take the bundles.

"Your grain!" replied Crow. "Who ever heard of anyone leaving bundles of grain by the roadside? Nonsense! This grain is mine."

Then Crow picked up the bundles and flew off with them. Greedy Spider and his wife and children returned home sad and empty-handed.

Their stealing had done them no good. Someone had taken from them what they had taken from another.

The Stone-Cutter

When Taro was a little boy, he said, "If I ever grow up to be a stone-cutter and can go up with the men in the morning and cut the great rocks from the mountainside, I shall be happy."

Years went by, and Taro grew big and strong. One morning, he took his hammer and set out with the men to climb the mountain and cut the rock from the mountainside.

It was a happy day for Taro. All day he swung his heavy hammer and laughed to see the great rock break and the chips fly about him. All day he worked in the hot sun, and he sang as he worked.

At nighttime, he came down the mountain, tired and happy. He was glad to eat his simple supper and go to bed. And so for many days he worked and sang.

But as time went on, he was not so happy. He grew tired of rising before the sun and climbing the mountain through the cold morning mist.

As he toiled, the hot sun beat down upon his back. The hammer **blistered** his hands. The sharp chips cut his face.

....

blistered caused raised sores

He no longer sang at his work. Taro was tired of being a
stone-cutter.

One day when he had a holiday, Taro went into
town. At noon he stopped to rest before a large house
that stood **in the midst of** beautiful rose gardens.

The door of the house opened and a man came out.
He was dressed in fine silks, as soft as spiders' webs and
colored like the rainbow. Jewels sparkled on his hands.
Taro watched him pick the roses and drop them into a
great basket carried by a servant at his side.

"Ah, me," said Taro to himself. "This must be a
very rich man."

....

in the midst of surrounded by

As he walked along the stony road that night, he looked at his blistered hands and thought of the rich man's jeweled fingers. When he came to his little hut at the foot of the mountain, he thought of the rich man's house in the midst of rose gardens.

He looked up at the mountain, where far above him the spirit of the mountain dwelt among the clouds and mists. He thought of how he must rise the next morning before the sun and climb up there to work all day in the burning heat.

"Oh, spirit of the mountain," cried Taro, "make me a rich man, too, so that I may wear silks as fine as spiders' webs, and live in a beautiful house, and walk in rose gardens. Then shall I be happy."

The spirit of the mountain heard and smiled. That very night, the little hut vanished. In its place stood a large house in the midst of rose gardens.

Taro was now a very rich man. He no longer had to rise before the sun and climb the steep mountainside. He no longer had to bend all day over his work while the hot sun beat down upon his head. He could walk all day in his rose garden if he wished. But he soon became very tired of it.

One day, as he stood looking out over his garden wall, a golden chariot came dashing by. It was drawn by six white horses with golden harnesses glittering in the sun. A **coachman** dressed in white and gold sat up on the seat in front and cracked a golden whip.

In the chariot sat a prince, dressed in purple and cloth of gold. Over his head there was a golden umbrella to shade him from the sun, and a servant ran beside him to fan him with a golden fan.

"So this is the prince," said Taro to himself. "He is far greater than I. He rules the land for miles about. He rides in a golden chariot with a golden umbrella over his head, and a servant fans him with a golden fan."

---

coachman someone who drives a carriage or coach

Then Taro cried to the spirit of the mountain, "Oh, spirit, I am tired of being a rich man and walking in my rose gardens. Make me a prince who rules the land. Let me ride in a golden chariot, with a golden umbrella over my head, and a servant to fan me with a golden fan. Then I shall surely be happy."

Again the spirit of the mountain heard and smiled, and again Taro had his wish.

In the blink of an eye, he became a prince. He lived in a fine palace. He had servants dressed in white and gold, and he rode in a golden chariot with a golden umbrella over his head. He ruled the country round about, and rich and poor obeyed him.

"There is no one so great as I am," he cried. "Now I am truly happy."

One hot summer day, Taro rode through his lands in his golden chariot. The flowers drooped by the wayside. The fields were dry and brown. He looked up at the hot sun that poured its rays upon the dry ground.

"The sun is greater than I am," cried Taro in sorrow. "Oh, spirit of the mountain, what pleasure is it to be a prince and rule the land and ride in a golden chariot with a golden umbrella over my head? The sun will not obey me. I wish I were the sun. Then I should indeed be happy."

In an instant, he was the sun. He laughed as he sent his rays down upon the backs of the poor stone-cutters on the mountain. He laughed as he saw the roses wither in the rich men's gardens and the princes try in vain to keep cool under their golden umbrellas.

"Ah, ha," he cried, as the earth turned brown and withered beneath his rays. "Now I am really happy. I am the strongest thing in the whole wide world."

But his happiness did not last. One day, a heavy cloud came between him and the earth. "Be gone," cried the sun, and shone its fiercest. But the cloud still floated before him.

"Be gone!" cried Taro. "Do you not see that I am the sun, the greatest thing in the world?" But still the cloud did not move.

"Alas!" cried Taro, "this cloud is greater than I. Let me be a cloud, spirit of the mountain, that I may be happy."

Once more the spirit of the mountain granted Taro's wish. He became a cloud. He hid the earth from the great sun and laughed at its rage. He sent cool showers upon the earth. The roses bloomed again. The fields grew green.

He laughed in joy at his power. He rained and rained till the rivers overflowed and the land was flooded.

Yet far up on the mountainside, the rocks stood firm. Try as he might, Taro could not move them. He poured **torrents** of rain upon them, but they did not stir. Because of this, Taro was not happy.

....

torrents rushes or very large amounts of water

"The rocks of the mountainside are mightier than I," he cried at last. "Oh, spirit of the mountain, let me be a rock, or I shall never be really happy."

The spirit of the mountain sighed a little. But it said, "Have thy wish. Be a rock."

It was pleasant to be a rock. The hot sun poured down its rays and the clouds dropped their rain, but the great rock stood firm. Even the prince in his golden chariot and the rich man in his rose garden could not have moved it. Surely, now Taro was happy. But his happiness did not last.

One day a man came to the mountain. Tap, tap, tap. The rock shivered as the hammer struck it. Tap, tap, tap. The rock split from side to side, and a great piece broke off and fell to the ground.

"Oh, spirit of the mountain," cried Taro in sorrow, "man is mightier than I. Change me once more to a man, and I shall be happy and contented."

Then the spirit of the mountain smiled. "Be thou a man," it said.

So Taro became a man again. He became once more the poor stone-cutter who lived at the foot of the mountain.

Every morning he rose before the sun and climbed the mountain through banks of mist. All day he bent over his work while the hot sun beat upon his head. In the evening, very tired, he climbed down the side and was glad to eat his simple supper and go to bed.

Yet Taro was happy. He had wished for many things and had tried them all. But in the end, he knew that the life of a stone-cutter suited him best.

Once more he laughed to see the great rock break and the chips fly. And once more he sang at his work.

The Bundle of Sticks

adapted from a fable by Aesop

There once was a man whose family argued **constantly**. He had tried in many ways to teach them not to quarrel but had failed.

One day, he called his sons together. He told them to lay a bundle of sticks before him. He tied a strong cord firmly around the bundle of sticks. He told his sons, one after the other, to take up the bundle and break it. They all tried, but they could not break the bundle.

Then the father untied the cord and gave his sons the sticks to break, one by one. They did this with the greatest ease.

Then the father said, "You are like the sticks, my sons. As long as you stand by each other, you are strong. You can do great things, meet any challenge, and stand up to any enemy. When you quarrel and separate, you are easily beaten. In **unity**, there is strength."

constantly without stopping
unity agreement on a purpose; being joined together as a whole

THE BUNDLE OF STICKS

The Necklace of Truth
A Play

adapted from the story by Jean Macé

Characters

NARRATOR

PEARL, a little girl who often tells lies

MOTHER, Pearl's mother

FATHER, Pearl's father

MERLIN, a wise wizard

COOK

ROSA, a neighbor of Pearl's

GIRLS

SETTING: *Long, long ago in England.*

Scene 1

The curtains rise on a large kitchen. At center stage is a large, heavy table with a plate of cookies sitting on it. An older woman is stirring a large pot on the stove. She is facing away from the cookies.

NARRATOR: There once was a little girl named Pearl, who had a bad habit of telling lies.

Pearl enters. She stuffs a handful of cookies into her pocket.

She immediately eats one and gets crumbs down the front of her dress.

COOK: Pearl, dear, did you just take some of the cookies?

PEARL: It was not I. I just saw a troll run through the kitchen and steal the cookies.

COOK: But, Pearl, I can see the crumbs on your dress.

PEARL: (*In a loud voice*) I tell you, I did not take the cookies! It was a troll!

Mother and Father enter the kitchen.

FATHER: What is all this noise I hear?

PEARL: I saw a troll steal the cookies, but Cook will not believe me.

MOTHER: Now, Pearl, there have not been trolls in the kingdom for many years now. That cannot be true.

NARRATOR: For a long time, Pearl's parents did not know of her bad habit. But at last they saw that she often said things that were not true.

FATHER: What shall we do? This bad habit of lying must end.

COOK: I have heard that the wise wizard Merlin is a friend of the truth. Children who go to him are often cured of this bad habit.

FATHER: Let us take our child to the wonderful wizard.

MOTHER: Yes, let us take her to Merlin. He will cure her!

Scene 2

Later that day. Father, Mother, and Pearl enter a grand room of Merlin's palace. Merlin is sitting in a large chair by the fire. The parents approach Merlin slowly, holding Pearl's hand. Pearl looks nervous.

MOTHER: Thank you for seeing us, sir. It's our daughter, Pearl. This is so difficult to say. She just...

MERLIN: I know very well what is the matter with her, my dear madam. Your child is one of the greatest liars in the world.

NARRATOR: How did Merlin know this? I cannot say, but this wizard could tell a liar, even though many miles away. And, Pearl? Upon hearing this, she hid her head with shame and fear.

MERLIN: (*Opens a drawer and takes from it a lovely necklace with a diamond clasp*) Do not be afraid, Pearl. I am only going to give you a present.

PEARL: (*Nervously*) Really?

....

clasp a kind of hook that holds two things together

MERLIN: (*Placing necklace around Pearl's neck*) Truly. Now, you must all go home and be happy. Your little girl will soon be cured of her bad habit.

FATHER: Thank you, Merlin. If you say so, it must be true.

MERLIN: (*Looking sternly at Pearl*) In a year from now, I shall come for my necklace. Till then you must not take it off—you must not dare take it off.

The next day in the garden of Pearl's home. Pearl is playing in the garden. Several neighbor Girls come by and gather around Pearl to look at her necklace.

NARRATOR: Now, this necklace Merlin gave Pearl was the wonderful Necklace of Truth.

ROSA: Oh, what a lovely necklace! Where did you get it, Pearl?

PEARL: My father gave it to me for a Christmas present.

NARRATOR: This, you know, was a **falsehood**.

GIRLS: (*Surprised*) Oh, look, look! The diamond has turned dim!

ROSA: The diamond clasp has changed to glass!

PEARL: (*In a shaky voice*) I will tell you the truth. The wizard Merlin gave it to me.

GIRLS: Look! The diamond is bright again.

ROSA: (*Laughing*) You were sent to Merlin for telling lies, weren't you?

PEARL: You need not laugh. Merlin sent a lovely coach to bring us. It was drawn by six white horses and was lined with satin and had gold tassels.

....

falsehood a lie

And his palace is all built of gems. And he praised me because I tell the truth.

NARRATOR: But these were all fibs, as you know. Pearl stopped, for the girls were laughing all the time she was speaking. Then she looked at her necklace—and what do you think? It hung down to the ground! With each lie she had told, the necklace had stretched more and more.

GIRLS: You are stretching the truth!

PEARL: I confess. All that I told you was false.

NARRATOR: At once the necklace changed to its right size.

ROSA: But what did Merlin say when he gave you the necklace?

PEARL: He said it was a present for a truthful—(*Gasps*)

NARRATOR: But Pearl could not go on speaking. The necklace had become so short that it nearly choked her.

PEARL: (*Sobbing*) Oh no! He said I was—I was—the greatest liar in the world.

NARRATOR: The girls did not laugh now. They were sorry for poor Pearl when they saw her weeping. So at last, Pearl was cured. She saw how wrong and how foolish it is to tell falsehoods.

Scene 4

One year later. Merlin enters Pearl's home.

MERLIN: As promised, I have come for my necklace. Does Pearl need to keep it any longer?

MOTHER: (*Happily*) Oh, no! Pearl has not told a falsehood for a good long while.

FATHER: Yes! She is a changed girl.

PEARL: Although the necklace is quite lovely, I will gladly return it to you. I have learned a great deal from this necklace.

MERLIN: Well, now there is a little boy who greatly needs my necklace. I am glad that you no longer need it.

PEARL: That is the truth. Never more will I tell a lie.

NARRATOR: And Pearl kept her word. So many years have passed since then that no one can tell where the wonderful Necklace of Truth might be. If it should ever be found, would you like to wear it? Would you always keep the diamond bright?

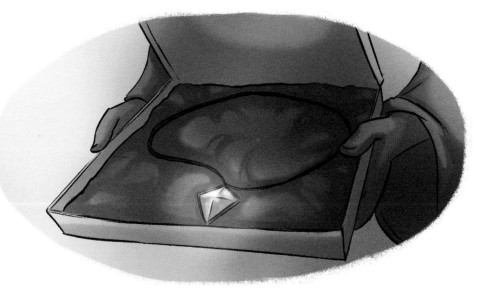

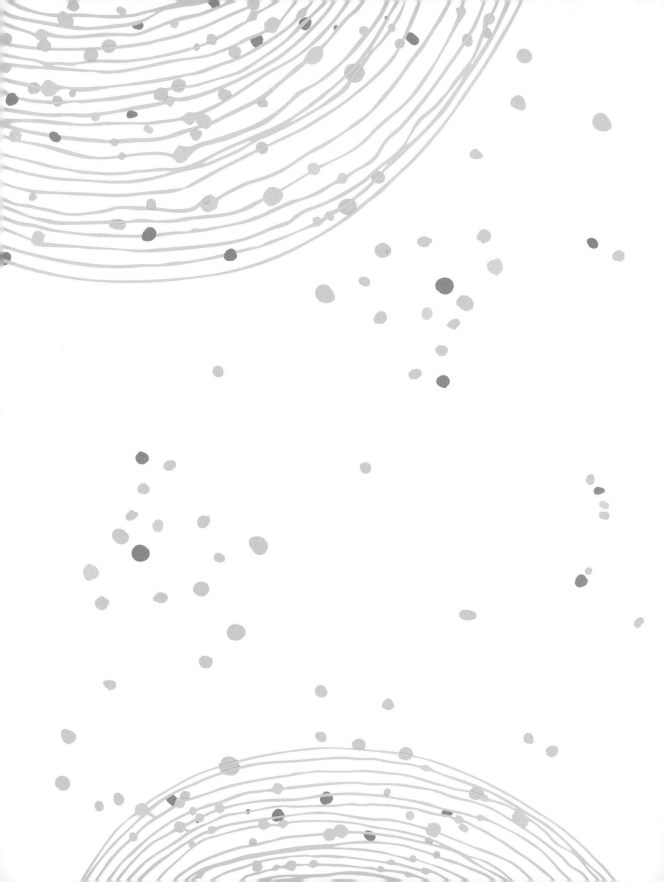